Layers

Ghst Writer

BookLeaf
Publishing

India | USA | UK

Presentation by *BookLeaf Publishing*

Web: www.bookleafpub.com

E-mail: info@bookleafpub.com

ISBN: 9789358313628

First edition 2024

To the ones I love that loved me back.

Thank you. xx

ACKNOWLEDGEMENT

To my friend (and spoken word artist) CD
Situation, thank you for being on the end of the
phone line through the writing process.
We started and completed this journey together
and despite a few technical issues we reached
the finish line!

Thank you Mum for raising me to see beauty in
everything and encouraging me to create art at
every opportunity. You also named me after a
poet, which I believe provided me with the
energy of a writer.

Thank you to my children, for being patient with
me and allowing me time and space to create
each day. You are growing into beautiful
humans.

And to that one special person who inspires me
to write daily and gives me the fearless energy I
need to overcome anything in life. Distance is
nothing energy is everything! You are more
special to me than you can comprehend.

Finally I need to thank God. There was a time I thought you didn't exist but you were here all along. I see you.

Love.

PREFACE

I read somewhere that the rapper J.Cole, inspired by the book 'The Artist's Way', would write three pages freehand every morning in a bid to overcome writers block.

Freehand is not usually something I commonly practice but writers block is way too familiar. When I decided to embark on this poetic journey my musical writers block was once again creeping in.

Poetry is a beautifully freeflowing artform that, although I have dabbled with it before, I have never fully immersed myself into creating.

I decided that, by writing each morning, without the tight structure of bars, flows and 16's, I could express my innermost thoughts freely and remain creatively stimulated during my break from music.

Every day I woke up and put my current thoughts and emotions onto paper and as time went on, I found poetry to be a safe space to express the little things I may never say out loud.

Through my eyes there is beauty in people.
Despite my frequent trips down the rabbit hole
of doubt in my own mind, I experience the
people I love on a highly spiritual level.

This collection of poems should give readers an
insight to the methods behind the madness that
is me!

As my good friend told me yesterday 'There's
layers to this s**t!'.

GHST
X

Grounded

Your surroundings
Do not define you
Stay grounded

Do not allow compromise
You stand for something
While others sit and allow themselves
To bow to that which is designed
To break our spirits

You are the embodiment of truth
The embodiment of strength and love
It radiates through your flesh into your aura
You are unmatched

A warrior that has won many battles
And came out merely scarred
And you have the heart
To win this one

Cos your surroundings
Do not define you!
Stay grounded.

Him (Part 1)

I can feel his soul
Thats where heaven lies
The connection transcends space and time
It's not his nor mine

It belongs to the universe
Created by God
It can only be divine
The frequency of love
Elevated to a new high

Outside of the physical body
Through the barriers of bricks and steel
No distance or door
Can interfere with true alignment
Freedom versus confinement

We sit on opposite sides
but we are one in the same
So complex yet so simple
My mirror image
Identical flames

Mind Over Matter

They say mind over matter
But for me
When it comes to matters of the heart
It's like my mind doesn't matter

You see love always gets me in trouble
I forget myself
I lose all logic
And no one can tell me
Stop it!

Not gonna lie
It's a problem
One that I can't seem to solve
Until I'm knee deep in f**kry

I never weigh up my options
I just run with it
No limit
Tryna master peace
But my souls different
Cos when it's lit up
With emotion I just
Get up and flow with it...

Like an ocean...

Swept up in devotion...

Bought into the notion...
That this is indeed the one

And I can't hear nothing but his song
And even though theres that niggling muffled
Doubt tryna shout from within saying
"Ghst you're wrong!"

I choose matter over mind...
Every time.

Peace

So long I have been searching
Not realising these external things I worship
Can't nurture what I search for
As its purpose is internal
And I'm still on that journey
After all
I deserve it

I know that I'm worthy I just need to
reach that little bit further
Within
The balance of both yang and yin
In perfect harmony
I have to ask myself why?
Why did you keep this so far from me?
When you knew it was in reach

It's always been part of me
I embody it in my artistry
Writing about our history
Releasing that pain through the ink
To the sheet
Cos that's where
I find
Peace.

Blind Eye

Sometimes I wonder why
The Universe would place
Something so amazing in my reach
Only to keep it at bay

It this a blessing or a curse
A lesson or even worse
Is this another karmic cycle
Designed to hurt
That I have turned a blind eye to

See trusting your intuition is vital
Dont ignore the premonitions be mindful
Your minds eye is insightful
And the feeling of love is so delightful
That you get swept away from the truth
That you have been seeking
All along.

Love

I love without expectation
Love is just an entire appreciation
Of who you are
Your mind and all within it
Your soul and spirit
Can we grow from these humble beginnings?
Love is an expression
Of my admiration and gratitude
For allowing me to experience
Your world

I listen in amazement
To your wisdom and your creations
I don't need persuading
That this is indeed
Love in full effect
Submerging me deeper
Each moment that passes
Each new thing I discover.

I love you.

Freefalling

That familiar feeling of dread
That rush in my chest
Stepping into unknown territory

Fear takes over
So many questions
So many doubts

Are you the same when I'm not around?
What you say in private will you say it loud?
And does she really know her place or have you
allowed her to step over that mark?

I know it's all a question of faith
Events I can't see
Judgements I can't make
I feel to put on the brakes
Cos right now I'm free falling
And there is so much at stake

Is this yet another mistake?
To add to my list of fucked up traits
That led me to nowhere but pain and heartache?

That I couldn't take

All I can do is pray

Dear God
Please don't let this be fake
I have ached enough in relationships
But I just can't bring myself to pull away
So I guess the truth will have to prevail.

Desire

The way I yearn for you
Is unexplained

You bear water
I am Earth
I need you to pour into me
So I can flourish
I receive
You nourish

The desire
Running wild
I feel it in my veins
And I have to restrain myself

Do not touch
Just observe
My mind tells me
Just observe
This perfect human being
In the flesh
And pretend you don't want to touch
Every single part of this...
Creation
That you patiently wait on

Body aching

Creating
Its own water
Everytime
You gaze
In his direction
Dissecting
Every section
Of his
Sensually
Sexually
Dominating
Prescence.

Selflessness

Selflessness is a trait of mine
That I need to learn to practice without
expectation
Cos I get deflated when I really need someone
But no one shows their face

You see I'm not one to cry out for help but if I do
it's cos I don't wanna break and in that moment
I'm debating my fate

And I remember all those times I helped carry
the weight but...
When there's too much on my plate no one came
and ate

I don't know whether selflessness is something I
embrace or hate
I should learn from my mistakes
Cos I don't rate the way the situation plays out
everytime

And I am well aware that I'll always be fine in
the end but why can't I learn to put myself first
Prioritise my self worth
Before I get hurt

It's a vicious cycle only I can say bye to
Striving to be mindful and trust my insight
before hindsight presents itself along with that
bitter regret...

Guess I need to live and let.

Affirmative

You can not cage energy
The physical union may be pending
But union has already commenced

In spirit, in love
Connected by mind
And soul
You can't take away
This gift

They see wrong
We know right
Out of sight
Never mind

I can't lie
I have been provoked to the point
Of rage
And at this stage I question...
Is this all worth it?

And somehow you show up
Through the flood of my tears
Just to tell me...

Yes.

Go with the flow

Do you believe in magic?
I gotta ask it cos
I do..

I know the connection
Telepathic, reflective
But something tells me
You are deflecting slightly
Maybe rejecting the idea
Of this higher power that is ours...

Or maybe I am overthinking again
My favourite pasttime as we both know
Down the rabbit hole I love to go...
No I don't think so to be honest
You know what I think?

I think you like to be in control instead of
Just...
Letting go

And sometimes we let our ego overflow
And block our own blessings
I should know

I have been the master of stunting my own
growth
But now I understand I can't hold onto ego
And reach my spiritual goals
It's a big NO!

I know what I know...
And as hard as it is
I have to let go of fear..
And go with the flow.

Otherwordly

I am tired and weary
But it can't beat me
It can't beat us
I am not yet defeated

You see I was built for battle
I was built to rise after every attempt
To make me fall
Each attempt to break me from within
Has resulted in growth

I will not leave anything unspoken
I am not from this world of trinkets and tokens
The things I possess do not equate to the value
of my soul
My mind is open

The fact is
It's systematic
We are surrounded by
conditioned actors
Playing their part in this
Actual simulation
Designed to break me
To break us

But they have not yet discovered
That we are
Otherworldly beings.

Shortie

Allowing yourself to feel
Will allow you to heal
I know you've been avoiding pain
Cos I know when it gets too real
It's easier to retreat rather than reveal your
wounds

I've been in your shoes
Hurt... bruised
Building walls so I can get through
Each day without anyone having a clue
That I'm in pain
I can't let no one gain power by seeing me
vulnerable
Can't fully let anyone in

Emotions buried in the rubble of the fast life
Intoxication and carnal pleasures...
Never one wife
Always on edge
Waiting for betrayal
As you can't trust a soul
One day it all comes to blows
And you...
You gotta just go with the flow

Reap what you sow
Pick it all apart and get to know...
You

And please don't take this as judgement
Cos I am you too
I'm writing with love and care
Cos I understand what you have had to bear
I've been there...
And now I'm here

By your side
No strings or ties
No ego or pride
Just holding you down
While you take those strides
And both of us get closer
To the light
Cos believe it or not
You're teaching me too
Thats the truth
I've been through this
On the other side
My eyes are open wide
And my heart is open wider
I get it all now Shortie
I got you always.

Survival Mode

Despite the distance
I can feel your embrace
Your energy makes me feel safe
Safe from harm and judgement
I feel your arms around me
From beyond the walls
I feel it all

Your energy wrapped around me protecting me
from myself
Protecting me from my fears
Creating that space for the awakening of that
Divine Feminine
Suppressed energy
That I have been protecting
With my own masculine force field
But whats weird is that
You took down Goliath
Cos that energy was giant
No match for most mortals
But you saw behind it
In a way even I declined to
Cos I was always confined to a space that felt
safe

And you know how it is we gotta survive out
here!
Playing in survival mode
You know the code!

I guess Goliath didn't get the memo
That this is the soft girl era

I don't need
That sword
That shield
Exit survival
This new phase is called...
THRIVING
And I'm about to dive in
Because I know SHE!
Is powerful enough
To survive it.

Triggered

Tryna control my mind
But the spiral is endless
And there is no sentence
You can say to help this
Sorry but
You're defenceless

Cos when this bull sees redness
I remain fixated
And it takes over my body and soul
Its infectious
Meditation aint helping
I try to tell myself
Stop being selfish
But I can't help it
I'm jealous

Tryna supress the menace to society
That I have been since I was about
10 or something
And the funny thing is that
It's always love that reconnects us

She is the teacher and I'm the apprentice
I just skip happily into battle mode

F**k friendship
When she knocks on for me to play out
I'm born ready
Come on Shelley
Let's go

You

I love you because
You simply exist
Inside all this chaos
You are a pillar of peace

You are a source of energy
When I am close to defeat
You are my inspiration
As I write to the beat

You are the catalyst
To my creative flow
You are the motivation I need
To reach my goals

You are my armour
When I face the war
You are my strength
In moments of weakness

But you are also
My weakness
Because I can't exist without
Your existence.

Seedling

Seedling
Growing into a beautiful flower
Graceful and full of wonder
Absorbing every aspect of the world around you

Inspired by sunrise and sunsets
Intrigued by words and colours
Making sense of self
Embracing your beauty and ability
Radiating love and innocence

You amaze me flower
Reaching towards the sun
As I tend to your roots
Pouring into you daily
Keeping you safe from harm
Watching you grow.

Him (Part 2)

Love can find you
In the strangest of places
When its last on your list
Of expectations
You're going about your day to day
Then suddenly your faced with...
Him

And it's funny cos he has always been there
You just ignored the feeling
Of needing to protect him
From the pain you saw in his eyes
The increasing speed of your heartbeat
When he speaks
The way that his appearance
Makes you feel weak
The way you need to be in his presence
Just to absorb a piece
Of his energy

You play down the fact you are
A little too over friendly
And it's not out of character for you
To sing so many melodies
But...

It's been a while
Just saying

You say his name when you're praying
He appears in your dreams when
You're laying your head down at night
Silently wishing he was next to you...
Right?

So was this really so sudden?
Or was it there all along
Orchestrated by God
His purpose divine
Another lesson disguised
Another opportunity
To fall or to rise.

Crazy

I have come to the conclusion
That I am crazy
I am completely unhinged
I am yet to make sense of
The workings of my mind
What is the filtering process
Can someone please explain?

Because logically B comes after A
But to get from A to B.. I
Seem to C
Its not OK
To go straight to my destination
Creating complications
Then look back and realise
That didn't need to be as hard as I make it

Guess I'm scared of being vulnerable
Stripped naked
But wait a minute
Y do I hate it so much?
That's where the growth happens
Where the character is built
Not from avoidance but from facing yourself
Head on... in your truest form.

Grateful

I am so grateful
That you came into my life
You allowed me to feel
So in turn I can heal

You knocked down the walls
Built with so much care and precision
They took years to build
You destroyed them in an instant
Revealing my essence and core
My vulnerabilities on display for all
The crazy thing is I'm not scared anymore

I have been freed from the chains that
Enslaved me blocking my greatness
And you have now paved the way for
My elevation and there is nothing more
That I wanna do
Than elevate in the presence of you.

One

Be careful what you speak into existence
As your persistance will grant your wishes
We can manifest anything we desire
Our power is higher than we are conditioned to
believe...

We are taught to grieve for that which we don't
possess keeping us in the mindset of lack

We romanticise a life that...
Provides us with prizes that keep us sidetracked
from the answers
The real rewards that will enhance us

Love.. Community...
Integrity... Unity...
Instead when the money tune plays we turn into
dancers
So knackered when we get home
We just scroll for the banter
Mindless chatter
With people that don't matter

We neglect the nourishment that our soul needs
We forget our brain needs to feed

Sometimes we go as far as to compromise our
morals for greed
Instead of sowing the seeds to succeed as one

We are mourning instead of raising suns
Another child gone
In the name of money and fun?
Come on!

Wake up!
So much at stake can we create a bond?
Cos we seem to have forgotten that we are one...

We are one!

www.ingramcontent.com/pod-product-compliance
Lightning Source LLC
La Vergne TN
LVHW041247200726
843507LV00013B/2851